FANTASTIC
JOKES

ARCTURUS

ARCTURUS

This edition published in 2013 by Arcturus Publishing Limited
26/27 Bickels Yard, 151–153 Bermondsey Street,
London SE1 3HA

Author: Tracey Turner
Illustrator: Peter Coupe
Editor: Becca Clunes

ISBN: 978-1-78212-390-3
CH003715EN
Supplier 03, Date 0413, Print run 2653

Printed in China

Contents

What's the difference between a train
and a teacher?

**A train says 'choo-choo' but a teacher says 'take
that gum out of your mouth this instant'!**

Why do teachers never marry dairy farmers?

They are like chalk and cheese!

How does a maths teacher remove wax
from his ears?

He works it out with a pencil!

TEACHER, TEACHER

Why did the Cyclops have to retire from teaching?

He only had one pupil!

Why do doctors enjoy their schooldays?

Because they are good at examinations!

Why are you taking that sponge
into your lesson?

I always find history such an absorbing subject!

Why did the scruffy schoolboy finally take a bath?

Because he realised that grime doesn't pay!

What do history teachers do before they get married?

They go out on dates!

A bottle of lemonade went to teacher training college.

He wanted to teach fizzical education!

Katie, name five things that contain milk!

Yogurt, cheese, and three cows!

Why did the maths teacher take a ruler in his car?

So he could see how long it took him to get to work in the morning!

What happened after the wheel was invented?

It caused a revolution!

How can you tell when a robot teacher is going mad?

He goes screwy!

Ella, why do you stare into space for hours?

I'm practising to be an astronomer!

You had better behave in Mr Simkins' music class, or you'll find yourself in treble!

Where would I find Offa's Dyke?

I think you should be asking Offa that question, Miss, not me!

Did you hear about the science teacher who was always playing tricks on people?

He was a real particle joker!

Carol, can you give me a sentence
with deliberate in it?

**'My dad bought a new settee and tomorrow
they are going to deliberate to our house!'**

Aidan, how would you discover what life
in Ancient Egypt was really like?

I'd ask my mummy!

Today we are going to look for the lowest
common denominator.

**Haven't they found it yet? My dad says they were
looking for that when he was at school!**

Did you hear about the maths teacher
whose mistakes started to multiply?

They took him away in the end!

Why are you always late for school?

It's not my fault, you always ring the bell before I get here!

Patrick, why is your homework late?

Sorry, Miss, my dad is a slow writer!

Philip, why do you always have two plates of food for school dinner?

It's important to have a balanced diet, Miss!

Mary, how did you find the questions in your
English exam?

**Oh, I found the questions easily enough.
It's the answers I couldn't find!**

DID YOU HEAR ABOUT ...

. . . the P.E. teacher who used to run
around the exam room in the hope of
jogging pupils' memories?

. . . the maths teacher and the art teacher
who liked painting by numbers together?

. . . the craft teacher who used to have the
class in stitches?

. . . the science teacher who was scared of
little glass dishes – he was Petri-fied?

. . . the cookery teacher who thought
Hamlet was an omelette served
with bacon?

William, how fast does light travel?

**I don't know, Sir, it's already arrived
by the time I wake up!**

Why did the school canteen hire a dentist?

To make more filling meals!

Jane, what do you know about the Dead Sea?

I didn't even know it had been poorly, Sir!

Sophie, do you understand how important
punctuation is?

**Yes, Miss, I always make sure I get to school
on time!**

I hope I don't catch you cheating in the
maths exam!

So do I, Miss!

Mandy, do you have to come to school chewing gum?

**No, Sir, I can stay at home and chew it
if you prefer!**

Fred, I told you to write 100 lines because your
handwriting is so bad, but you have only done 75!

**Sorry, Miss, but my maths is just as bad
as my handwriting!**

Why did the school orchestra have such
awful manners?

Because it didn't know how to conduct itself!

Why do school cooks make good
history teachers?

**They know more than anyone else about
ancient grease!**

Ghostly Goings-on

What sport did Frankenstein's monster compete in?

The pole volt!

Why did the vampire go to the doctor's?

He needed something for his coffin!

Baby Monster: When I grow up I want
to drive a tank!

**Mummy Monster: Well, I certainly won't stand
in your way!**

What sort of monster drinks tinned blood?

A canpire!

What should you do after shaking hands
with a monster?

Count your fingers!

Who do zombies invite to their parties?

Anyone they can dig up!

What do you call a blood-sucking bat
that attacks pigs?

A hampire!

Did you hear about the mummy who wanted
to be a rock star?

He started his own rock bandage!

What do ghostly police officers do?

They haunt down criminals!

What sort of monster lives in your hanky?

A bogeyman!

Which monster is the most untidy?

The Loch Mess Monster!

Why do monsters make good fashion models?

**Because no matter what they are wearing
they always look so ghoul!**

What does a monster call knights in armour?

Tinned food!

What do vampires use to phone relatives?

A terror-phone!

How do vampires get clean?

In a blood bath!

Did you hear about the ghost who cut down trees
at three o'clock in the morning?

He was the thing that made stumps in the night!

What noise do baby witches make when they're
playing with toy cars?

Broom, broom!

Who do vampires invite to their weddings?

All their blood relatives!

Why was the monster catching centipedes?

He wanted scrambled legs for breakfast!

What is the difference between a ghost
and a custard cream biscuit?

Have you tried dipping a ghost in your tea?

What do you call a ghost in armour,
haunting your roof?

A knight on the tiles!

What does Dracula have fitted to the front
of his car?

Head-vamps!

Which monster ate the three bears?

Ghouldilocks!

Did you hear about the vampire burglar
who was caught red-handed?

They caught him fang to rights!

Why do vampires have a steady nerve?

They are as ghoul as cucumbers!

Why do zombies always look so tired?

They are dead on their feet!

If you're good at writing, Dracula has
a job for you.

**He's looking for someone to answer his fang mail,
and become his crypt writer!**

What did the blacksmith
do when he saw
Frankenstein's
monster's neck?

He made a bolt for it!

How do you get a message
to a deep sea monster?

Drop him a line!

Why was the sea monster wet?

Because the seaweed!

In the monster version of the story of Snow White,
what are the seven dwarves called?

Snacks!

21

Who was the fattest mummy ever?

Two ton Khamun!

Who do you phone to rent a Dracula costume?

Vamp-hire!

What do you get if you cross a vampire
with a robot?

Something new-fangled!

Did you hear about the two ghosts that
got married?

It was love at first fright!

What does a vampire write with?

A Pencil-vania!

What pop group did the young
mummies join?

A boy bandage!

How do vampires start a duel?

They stand Drac to Drac!

What do skeleton teachers say at the start
of the lesson?

As there is nobody here we can start!

How did the ghostly teacher make sure his pupils had learned what he had written on the blackboard?

He went through it again!

What can you use to flatten a ghost?

A spirit level!

What do you call a dentist who really likes vampires?

An extractor fan!

What do you call a lazy skeleton?

Bone idle!

Why do ghosts go back to the same place every year for their holidays?

They like their old haunts best!

Where in America do monsters go
for their holidays?

Death Valley!

What do monsters like to pour on their
Sunday dinner?

Grave-y!

What do you call a vampire that you can dip into
your tea?

Count Dunkula!

What did the pirate get when he smashed
a skeleton up in a fight?

A skull and very cross bones!

What do the police call it when they watch
a vampire's house?

A stake out!

What pets does Dracula own?

A blood hound and a ghoul-fish!

What do you call a ghostly teddy bear?

Winnie the Oooooooooooohhhhhhh

What villain does the spooky 007 fight?

Ghoulfinger!

What do skeletons learn about at school?

Decimals and fractures!

What do skeletons learn about at school?

Why didn't the skeleton fight the monster?

He didn't have the guts!

What does a young boy ghost do to get a girlfriend?

He wooooooooooooos her!

Why are owls so brave at night?

Because they don't give a hoot for ghosts, monsters or vampires!

What do mummies do to relax?

They just unwind a little!

Why was the mummy's leg stiff?

Because someone had been winding him up!

Why are mummies good at keeping secrets?

They can keep things under wraps for centuries!

Who was the winner of the headless horse race?

No one, they all finished neck and neck!

What eats your letters when you post them?

A ghost box!

Which creature saves people from drowning?

The ghost guard!

Why did the vampire like eating chewy sweets?

He liked something to get his teeth into!

Why are sausages scared when they are
being cooked?

Because it's a terror-frying experience!

Why can you never get through to a vampire bat
on the telephone?

Because they always hang up!

What do monsters eat at tea time?

Scream cakes!

What do you call a vampire mummy?

Wrapula!

What do you call a young skeleton in a cap and uniform?

A skullboy!

Why did the witch take her small book of magic on holiday?

The doctor told her to get away for a little spell!

How does a skeleton know when it's going to rain?

He just gets a feeling in his bones!

Why do sea monsters go to so many parties?

They like to have a whale of a time!

What do baby sea monsters play with?

Doll-fins!

Why was the vampire lying dead
on the floor of the restaurant?

It was a stake house!

What do you give a monster
that feels sick?

Plenty of room!

Why did the ghost go to the bicycle shop?

**He needed some new spooks for
his front wheel!**

What was Dr Frankenstein best at?

Making new friends!

What do spooks eat in the morning?

A hearty breakfast of Dreaded Wheat!

What do you get if you cross the Abominable
Snowman and Count Dracula?

Severe frostbite!

Where do spooks go shopping?

In BOOOO-tiques!

What do Italian monsters eat?

Spook-ghetti!

What happens when a witch catches
the flu?

Everyone gets a cold spell!

What is Frankenstein's monster's worst nightmare?

**Being in a room full of people – without
a stitch on!**

Who delivers Christmas presents to vampires?

Sack-ula!

Which water monster swims about
in his underwear?

The Loch Vest Monster!

What do you get if you cross a vampire
with a petrol pump?

**Something that makes a hole in your car
and sucks out all the petrol!**

How do vampires show affection
for each other?

They bat their eyelids!

What should you say when a vampire
gives you a present?

Fang you very much!

Why should you never invite monsters
to a housewarming party?

Because they bring flame throwers!

What game do ghostly mice play at parties?

Hide and Squeak!

Where would you find a suitable gift
for a ghost?

In a chain store!

Werewolf Howlers

What sort of voice do werewolves have?

Husky ones!

What do you call a lost hairy monster?

A where-am-I wolf!

What do you call a lost hairy monster?

Did you hear about the werewolf who dropped his trousers?

Well – it was a full moon!

What do you call an escaped hairy monster?

A where's-he-gone wolf!

How do monsters eat their dinner?

They wolf it down!

If hairy palms is the first sign of turning into
a werewolf, what is the second?

Looking for them!

What sort of jokes do werewolves like best?

Howlers!

What happens when a werewolf meets
a vampire?

He doesn't turn a hair!

What sort of news do werewolves fear?

Silver bulletins!

What room must all werewolf homes have?

A changing room!

Why did the shy werewolf hide in a cupboard every full moon?

Because he didn't like anyone to see him changing!

What do you get if you shoot a werewolf with a silver bullet?

A very interesting rug!

What market do werewolves hate going to?

The flea market!

What did the werewolf say to the vampire?

'It's been nice getting to gnaw you!'

What form of self defence do werewolves use?

Coyote!

How do you stop a werewolf attacking you?

Throw a stick for it to fetch!

What sort of wolf can you wear?

A wear wolf!

Daddy, daddy, what's a werewolf?

Be quiet and comb your face!

What do you call a werewolf in a desert?

A hot dog!

Foolish
Folly

Where did the stonemason take his girlfriend?

To a rock concert!

Where did the fizzy-drinks maker take
his girlfriend?

To a pop concert!

Waiter, can I have my lunch on the patio?

**Certainly, sir, but most people find a plate
more sensible!**

Why did the idiot swallow a bag full of pennies?

**Because he thought the change would
do him good!**

Why should you never tell secrets in a corn field?

Because you're surrounded by ears!

Did you hear about the magician's family?

He had one half-brother and one half-sister!

Did you hear about
the posh chef with an
attitude problem?

**He had a French-fried
potato on his shoulder!**

Mmmm!
This jam sponge cake
is lovely and warm!

**It should be, the cat's been
sitting on it all afternoon!**

Why did the robot need
a manicure?

He had rusty nails!

Why were the naughty eggs sent out of the class?

For playing practical yolks!

Why did the bakers work late?

Because they kneaded the dough!

Why did the carpenter go to the doctor?

He had a saw hand!

What can you hold but never touch?

Your breath!

Why did the man jump up and down after taking his medicine?

Because he forgot to shake the bottle before he took it!

Why did the idiot apply for a job as a language teacher?

Because someone told him he spoke perfect rubbish!

What are dog biscuits made from?

Collie-flour!

What do you get if you cross a bird with a snake?

A feather boa constrictor!

If I cut a potato in two, I have two halves.
If I cut a potato in four, I have four quarters. What
do I have if I cut a potato in sixteen?

Chips!

Did you hear about the sculptor's son?

He was a chip off the old block!

What's the difference between margarine
and a goat?

You mean you can't tell margarine from butter?

What does it mean if your nose starts to run?

It's trying to catch a cold!

Why should you always be thankful to pigs?

**Because you should never take them
for grunted!**

What do sea monsters eat?

Fish and ships!

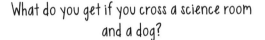

What do you get if you cross a science room
and a dog?

A Lab!

What do you call the place where all the
used lottery tickets are thrown?

The National Littery!

What happened when two wasps had a fight?

There was a terrible BUZZZTUP

What do you call a worm in a fur coat?

A caterpillar!

Why is Cinderella so bad at football?

**She has a pumpkin for a coach, and she keeps
running away from the ball!**

What insect do you find before the sea?

The B!

Why didn't the vampire laugh at the joke
about the wooden stake?

He didn't get the point!

What do you get from a nudist pig?

Streaky bacon!

A load of bees were getting very hot and
bothered one summer's day, and the queen bee
asked what the trouble was.

The bees just said, 'S'warm!'

What did zero say to eight?

Nice belt!

Where do they keep old cows?

In a Mooo-seum!

What is always dressing?

Mayonnaise!

Where do space monks live?

In a Moon-astery!

How do ducks play tennis?

With a quacket!

In the olden days, false teeth were made
of wood. Which tree did the wood
come from?

The gum tree!

What do you give a pig with a sore bottom?

Oinkment!

What did the careful robot say?

Look before you bleep!

Why did the monster eat a settee
and two armchairs?

He had developed a suite tooth!

Why did the vampire bats hanging in the church belfry look exactly the same as each other?

They were dead ringers!

How many letters in hungry horse?

Four: MTGG!

Why was the genie in the lamp angry?

Someone rubbed him up the wrong way!

What is red and cheeky?

Tomato sauce!

What do you get if you cross a space suit
and a saddle?

A horse-tronaut

Why are vampires so stupid?

Because blood is thicker than water!

Why do flamingoes stand on one leg?

Because if they lifted both legs they would fall over!

Which age did Egyptian mummies live in?

The Band-Age!

How many sheep does it take to
make a sweater?

Wow – I didn't even know sheep could knit!

Why did the idiot fall asleep in a bakery?

He went there for a long loaf!

Waiter, waiter, this lemonade is cloudy!

No it isn't, sir, it's the glass that's dirty!

Why did the burglar break into the
music shop?

He was after the lute!

What do you call a man with a speedometer
on his head?

Miles!

Waiter, waiter, there's a fly in my soup!

Sorry, madam, I didn't know you were vegetarian!

What's the special offer at the pet shop this week?

Buy one cat, get one flea!

What's bright red, has two wheels, runs on petrol and eats cornflakes?

A motorbike – I lied about the cornflakes!

Why did the burglar buy a surf board?

He wanted to start a crime wave!

Did you hear about the dog who was arrested?

He forgot to pay a barking ticket!

What do you call a pimple on a Tyrannosaurus Rex?

A dino-sore!

When do two and two make more than four?

When they make 22!

A bird in the hand . . .

Is likely to poo on your wrist!

Why should you never listen too closely
to the match?

Because you might burn your ears!

How does Father Christmas begin a joke?

This one will sleigh you . . .!

What did the bull say when he came back from
the china shop?

I had a really smashing time!

Did you know this is a one-way street?

I'm only going one way!

Yes, but everyone else is going the other way!

**Well, you're a police officer, make them
turn round!**

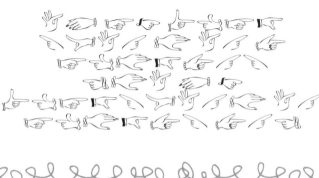

Potty
Poems

I wandered lonely as a cloud
That floats on high o'er hill and dell.
No-one would sit next to me
'Cos I'd made a nasty smell!

Mary had a little lamb,
and a little pony, too.
She put the pony in a field,
and the lamb into a stew!

POTTY POEMS

Humpty Dumpty sat on a wall,
Humpty Dumpty had a great fall.
All the king's horses and all the king's men
Thought it was really funny,
And asked him to do it again!

I went to the pictures tomorrow,
I got a front row seat at the back,
I bought an ice cream with a cherry on top,
I ate it and gave it them back!

Little Miss Muffet
Sat on her tuffet
Eating her favourite lunch.
A giant went by
Looking up to the sky
And Little Miss Muffet went 'CRUNCH'

Hickory Dickory Dock,
Six mice ran up the clock.
The clock struck one,
But the other five
got away!

Little Jack Horner
Sat in the corner,
Eating his apple pie.
He put in his thumb
and pulled out a plum,
And said, 'That's
a funny looking apple!'

POTTY POEMS

Jack and Jill
Went up the hill
To fetch a pail of water,
Jack fell down
And broke his crown
And Jill said,

'I told you you shouldn't try
and skateboard down!'

I never could quite work out why
An elephant could never fly.
With massive ears to flap and twitch
You'd think they'd glide without a hitch.

There was a lady from Crewe,
Who found a dead mouse in her stew,
The waiter said, "Don't shout and wave it about,
The others will want one too!"

I once met a man from Hong Kong
Who'd been jogging for twenty years long.
He was terribly sweaty,
He looked like a yeti,
And his feet had a terrible pong!

A rather dim gardener from Leeds
Once swallowed a packet of seeds.
In just a few weeks
His ears turned to leeks,
And his hair was a tangle of weeds!

Mary had a little fox,
It ate her little goat.
Now everywhere that Mary goes
She wears her fox-skin coat!

Who, What, Where, When and Why?

Why are you taking that shovel to your
singing class?

So I can get to the low notes!

Who runs the pub in the jungle?

The wine-ocerous!

Why did the cannibal go the wedding?

**Because he heard they were going
to toast the bride and groom!**

Why did the athlete run across everyone sitting
in the park?

**Because his trainer told him to run over
twenty laps!**

Why do doctors hate teachers when they come to
see them?

**Because they never give them enough time
to finish the examination!**

WHO, WHAT, WHERE,
WHEN AND WHY?

What sort of wallpaper do birds like best?

Flock!

I've got a giant pack of playing cards!

Big deal!

Why did Belinda give cough medicine
to the pony?

**Because Sally told her it was
a little horse!**

Waiter, waiter, why is this dead mouse
in my soup?

**Terribly sorry, sir, it should be
in the pudding!**

CREAM OF
MOUSEROOM
SOUP

Where do teachers get all their information?

From fact-ories!

What did one saltcellar say to the other saltcellar
when they made a deal?

Let's shake on it!

Why did the idiot drive his car off the side
of a mountain?

**Because someone told him that it was
fitted with air brakes!**

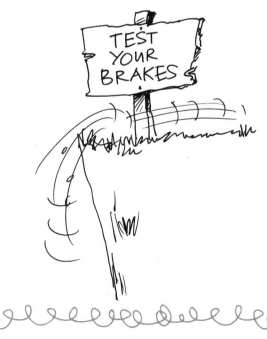

What do mice sing at birthday parties?

For cheese a jolly good fellow!

What does a toad use for making furniture?

A toad's tool!

What were the sixteen boys playing
in the telephone box?

Squash!

What work does Santa Claus do in the garden?

Ho ho hoeing!

What does it mean when the barometer falls?

**It means my dad is useless at knocking nails
into the wall!**

What do you call a prisoner's budgie?

A jail bird!

How do you wake chickens in the morning?

With an alarm cluck!

What do you call a man with soil on his head?

Pete!

Which famous knight never won a single battle?

Sir Rendor!

What creature sticks to the bottom
of sheep ships?

Baaa-nacles!

How do you know if your little brother
is turning into a fridge?

**See if a little light comes on whenever
he opens his mouth!**

Where do fish like going for their holidays?

Finland!

Where is the easiest place to find diamonds?

In a pack of cards!

Why is it easy to swindle a sheep?

**Because you can easily pull the wool
over its eyes!**

What do you get if you cross a brain surgeon
and a herd of cows?

Cow-operation!

What sort of fish would you find in a bird cage?

A perch!

What is a bunsen burner for?

Setting fire to bunsens!

What sort of fish would you find in a shoe?

An eel!

Why was the butcher worried?

His job was at steak!

Why did the doll blush?

Because she saw the teddy bear!

WHO, WHAT, WHERE, WHEN AND WHY?

What do you get if you cross a frog
and a fizzy drink?

Croaka-cola!

What do you call a German barber?

Herr Dresser!

Why do teddy bears never hear what
you say?

Because they have cloth ears!

What sort of ring is always square?

A boxing ring!

What sort of queue is always straight?

A snooker cue!

Why do people leave letters at the
football ground?

They want to catch the last goal-post!

Why do golfers carry a spare sock?

Because they might get a hole in one!

What do you get if you cross a pig with a hedgehog?

A porkupine!

Why did the doctor take his nose to pieces?

He wanted to see what made it run!

What is the name of the detective who sings quietly to himself while solving crimes?

Sherlock Hums!

Why did the farmer feed his pigs sugar and vinegar?

He wanted sweet and sour pork!

What do you call the Scottish dentist?

Phil McCavity!

What sort of chocolate bars do snowmen eat?

Snowflakes!

What kind of rose has a bark?

A dog rose!

Waiter, waiter, why is there a dead fly
in my soup?

**Well, you surely don't expect to get a live one
at these prices!**

What should you say to a giant ape who's won
the lottery?

'Kong-ratulations!'

What happened to the man who stole some eggs?

**He gave himself up – he said he only did it
for a yolk!**

What is most read at Christmas?

Rudolph's nose!

Why do cows have horns?

**Because they would look pretty silly
with bells on their heads!**

WHO, WHAT, WHERE, WHEN AND WHY?

What do you get if you cross a fruit
and a woman who needs help?

A damson in distress!

What do you get if you train a reindeer
to be a hairdresser?

Styling mousse!

Why was Dracula ill after biting someone
on a train home from work?

He caught a commuter virus!

What did the stupid burglar do when he saw a 'WANTED' poster outside the police station?

He went in and applied for the job!

What flowers do wasps like best?

Bee-gonias!

How do you grow a werewolf from a seed?

Just use plenty of fur-tiliser!

WHO, WHAT, WHERE, WHEN AND WHY?

Why did the fly fly?

Because the spider spied her!

Why did the Romans build straight roads?

They didn't want anyone hiding round the corners!

Why do police officers like discos?

They like a good steady beat!

What is the difference between electricity
and lightning?

Lightning is free!

What do you call a dinosaur that keeps you awake
at night?

Bronto-snore-us!

Where do vampires keep their savings?

**In the blood bank! (That's why they're
always in the red!)**

Alphabet Antics

A

Artichoke Joke that artists tell each other!

Address Book Large book where women keep their clothes!

Alarm clock Timepiece that scares everybody!

Appetite When you can't eat because your belt is too tight!

B

Baby Small bee!

Bank Side of river where voles keep their money!

Bark The sound a tree makes!

Bewitched Insect that has upset a witch!

C

Canary Bird that comes in a tin!

Cartoon Song you sing in the car!

Catapult Weapon used by cats!

Coconut Someone who loves cocoa!

D

Desert Pudding made from sand!

Dogma Mother of puppies!

Door catch Splinter that rips clothes when you go into house!

Dynamite Then again she might not!

E

Ear Opposite of there!

Electrician Someone who does tricks with light bulbs!

Escalator Moving stairway that makes you late for school!

F

False teeth Teeth that tell lies!

Fly paper What flies read to get the news!

Fortune cookie Expensive biscuit

Fur Type of woolly tree!

G

Gamble Lambs in a lottery!

Giant snails What you find on the end of giant's fingers!

Gnome A gnouse where elves live!

Greenhouse Home for aliens!

H

Hammock Bed for pigs!

Hippie One of the joints in your leggie!

Honeycomb What bees do their hair with!

Horse When a pony has a sore throat!

I

Icicle Bicycle with a wheel missing!

Inkling Baby pen!

J

Juggler Vein that Dracula visits the circus to see!

Jumper Cross between a sheep and a kangaroo!

K

Kippers Sleeping fish!

Knight What you get if you knit
with steel wool!

L

Ladybird Female bird!

Lighthouse What a snail carries on its back!

Lizard Magician in a snakes' circus!

Loaf What idle bread does!

M

Meatball What sausages play hockey with!

Monkey What an ape opens his door with!

Moth ball Dance where butterflies are
made welcome!

Mountaineer What a mountain listens with!

N

Nailbiter Monster with metal teeth!

Narrow squeak The noise you hear when you tread on a thin mouse!

Nervous wreck Sunken ship with a twitch!

Newspaper What gnus read!

O

Orangeade What you give a deaf fruit!

PARDON?!

P

Pane What you feel when you walk
into a sheet of glass!

Peanuts The sort of nuts you find in a pod!

Phoney Someone who pretends he has
a telephone in his pocket!

Porcupine Cross between a pig and
a tropical fruit!

Q

Quack Duck doctor!

Quicksand Builder's material that runs away
when you're not looking!

R

Reptile Flat lizards that stick to bathroom walls!

Road hog Pig who drives badly!

Roller skates Dangerous wheeled fish!

Rose petal What you have on a rose bicycle!

S

Skateboard Fish used as transport by sharks!

Soap Opera Singing in the bath or shower!

Spellbinding The covers on a witch's book!

Stork Creeping up behind a bird with long legs!

T

Tap dancer Someone who dances in the sink!

Tapeworms What insects use to measure things!

Time Herb with a wristwatch!

Toadstools What toads use for DIY!

U

Underpants Knickers worn in submarines!

Urine Where you are when you're not outside.

V

Vacuum cleaner Used to keep space nice and clean!

Varnish Disappear with a shiny finish!

Viper Snake used to clean car windscreen!

W

Warren A man who keeps pet rabbits!

Water polo Sport played on sea horses!

Witch doctor Person visited by sick witches!

X, Y, Z

X-Ray Used to belong to Ray!

Xylophone What xylos use to call their friends!

Yak Talkative animal!

Zombie Undead bee!

Sickly
Smiles

How do you keep flies out of your kitchen?

**Move the pile of rotting vegetables
into the lounge!**

Why are vampires good comedians?

They have a biting wit!

Why are vampires good comedians?

What does the cannibal plastic surgeon charge?

An arm and a leg!

How do bees qualify to make honey?

They have to pass their hiving test!

What are white, scary and enable you to open
any door?

Skeleton keys!

Did you hear about the monster who carried
on the family tradition?

He was swallowing in his father's footsteps!

Why is the soil in my garden
always dry?

Because you have leeks!

What do you call a baby budgie?

A budget!

Why do chickens listen to the radio?

**It's their only form
of hentertainment!**

What sort of teeth can sing in a high voice?

Falsetto teeth!

Why did the man send his alphabet soup back?

**Because he couldn't find words
to describe it!**

What sort of music can you listen to in bed?

Sheet music!

How do fleas train?

They have to start from scratch!

What do you call sheep who write to each other?

Pen friends

What is the only thing that you can lose
and yet still have?

Your temper!

What gets smaller the more
you put in it?

A hole in the ground!

What has fifty feet but can't walk?

A tape measure!

What has a hundred feet but can't walk
and isn't a tape measure?

A dead centipede!

Which profession gets most fringe benefits?

Hairdressing!

In which job do you get the most perks?

Working in a coffee shop!

What runs all day but is never short
of breath?

A train!

What sort of eggs go into uncharted areas
of the world?

Egg-splorers!

What is the difference between a blue elephant
and an apple?

Apples aren't blue!

What do you call a lion with toothache?

Rory!

What is huge, grey and has twelve feet?

Three elephants!

What driver has never passed a test?

A screwdriver!

What is the biggest mouse ever discovered?

The hippopotamouse!

What sort of holidays do cannibals
never go on?

Self-catering!

What do blacksmiths eat for breakfast?

Vice Crispies!

What do you get if you cross a giant monster
with a frog?

**Something that can catch planes with
its tongue!**

What do you call a baby insect's toy rabbit?

A bug's bunny!

What sort of shoes do frogs wear in summer?

Open toad sandals!

Why was the mother flea depressed?

All her children had gone to the dogs!

Why did the cannibal have indigestion?

He must have eaten someone who disagreed with him!

Did you hear about the guard dog that loved raw onions and garlic?

His bark was much, much worse than his bite!

What does a vegetarian cannibal eat?

Swedes!

Why do ghosts like going to shops that are having sales?

They enjoy bargain haunting!

What do dogs and trees have in common?

Bark!

A woman went into a pet shop and asked if she could have a hamster for her son.

'Sorry,' replied the shop keeper, 'we don't do part exchange!'

How do chickens tell their children off?

They say, 'Cock-a-doodle-don't do that!'

What is a big game hunter?

Someone who can't find the football stadium!

Why did the fish hire a removal van?

Because he was moving to a new plaice!

Did you hear about the man who ran away with
a deer to get married?

They anteloped!

What's a plumber's favourite vegetable?

Leeks!

Can you carry on playing football
during a flood?

Yes, you just have to bring on your subs!

What does a skeleton eat at a restaurant?

Ribs!

What is a prickly pear?

Two hedgehogs!

What do you call an elephant wearing rain boots?

A wellyphant!

What do bees do when they move into a new hive?

They have a house-swarming party!

Whenever I'm down in the dumps,
I buy myself some new clothes!

Ah! So that's where you get them from!

What do you get if you cross a cow with
a crystal ball?

A message from the udder side!

Which knight designed tombs?

Sir Cophagus!

Which famous artist invented fizzy drinks?

Lemonado Da Vinci!

Waiter, waiter, there are two worms on my plate!

They are the sausages, sir!

I got a puncture driving here today!

I told you to watch out for that fork in the road!'

SICKLY SMILES

What do you get if you cross a vampire
with a knight of the round table?

A bite in shining armour!

What do you give a sick snake?

Asp-rin!

Why do vampires like funerals?

Because every shroud has a silver lining!

Doctor, doctor, I feel like a goat!

Really? How are the kids?

What did the curtain say to the window?

'I've got you covered!'

Doctor, doctor, I've got an itchy, spotty
patch on my nose. Should I put cream on it?

Now, now, let's not do anything rash!

What do you get if you cross a carrier pigeon with
a woodpecker?

A bird that knocks before delivering a message!

What do you get if you cross a flock
of sheep and a radiator?

Central bleating!

Spaced Out

What lights do aliens switch on every Saturday?

Satellites!

What game do aliens play to while away
the hours in deep space?

Moonopoly!

What do you get if you cross a student
and an alien?

Something from another universe-ity!

How do you know when an alien is homesick?

He just moons about!

What do you give
a sick alien?

Planetcetamol!

Why did the attendant turn space ships
away from the lunar car park?

It was a full moon!

What sort of poetry do aliens like?

Uni-verse!

What do nasty aliens play with Earth spaceships?

They use them as shuttlecocks!

Where do aliens keep fish they capture
from other planets?

In a planetarium!

What do you call an alien who travels through space
on a ketchup bottle?

A flying saucer!

What do you call a sad space ship?

An unidentified crying object!

How does a Martian know he's attractive?

When bits of metal stick to him!

What do you call a space ship made from cow pats?

A Poo F O!

What do you call a space ship made from cow pats?

Why are alien gardeners so good?

Because they have green fingers!

How do you know if there is an alien
in your house?

**There will be a spaceship parked
in the garden!**

How do you catch a Venusian mega-mouse?

In a Venusian mega-mouse-trap!

What do aliens put on their cakes?

Mars-ipan!

What do alien children do on Halloween?

**They go from door to door dressed
as humans!**

Why did the alien buy honey and lemon juice?

He wanted a sweet and sour saucer!

What do Daleks drink?

Exterminade!

Where do Martians go to see a movie?

Cine-Mars!

What do you call a noisy space ship?

A space racket!

What do you get if you cross a compass and a shellfish?

A guided mussel!

Nutty Notions

What is furry and smells of mint?

A polo bear!

What do cats eat for breakfast?

Shredded Tweet!

What does Doctor Jekyll do on hoilday?

He tans his Hyde!

Which ancient leader was round and purple?

Alexander the Grape!

What do frogs drink at bedtime?

Croako!

What happened when the piano fell on the army barracks?

There was A flat Major!

What do you call a mad squirrel?

Nuts!

Who is the strongest man in the world?

**A policeman – he can hold up a whole street
full of traffic with one hand!**

What is big and grey and wobbly?

A jellyphant!

What is yellow and white and travels
at 125 miles an hour?

A train driver's egg sandwich!

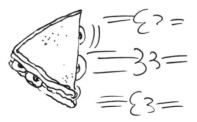

What goes oom, oom, oom?

A cow walking backwards!

Why was the idiot feeding his chickens haggis?

He wanted them to lay Scotch eggs!

How do you stop moles from digging up
your lawn?

Lock the toolshed!

What do you call a fish with four eyes?

Fiiiish!

What do you get if you cross a skunk
with a hot-air balloon?

Something that stinks to high heaven!

What is the only animal that can't hide?

The leopard, because it's always spotted!

What sort of snake will tell on you?

A grass snake!

How do you make a
sausage roll?

**Push it down a
steep hill!**

What do you call frozen mice?

Micicles!

What building drips cheese and tomatoes?

The leaning tower of Pizza!

Why couldn't Noah, his son and his wife all go fishing?

He only had two worms!

How do cavemen get to know each other?

By joining clubs!

When do kangaroos propose to one another?

During leap years!

What do you call a wizard on a broomstick?

A flying sorcerer!

What did the vampire doctor say?

Necks please!

Why were the carpenter's teeth chipped?

Because he was always biting his nails!

What do you get if you cross a dinosaur with a fish?

Jurassic shark!

Where do cats sleep?

On a caterpillar!

Did you hear about the orchestra leader
who survived being hit by lightning?

Fortunately he was a very bad conductor!

What do you find in an angry
sewing machine?

Cross stitches!

Waiter, waiter, there's a button in my lettuce!

Ah! That will be from the salad dressing sir!

Why do pens get sent to prison?

To do long sentences!

What's grey, weighs two and a half tons
and floats gracefully through the air?

A hang-gliding elephant!

What do you call an 85-year-old ant?

An antique!

What happens when there is a stampede
of cows on the motorway?

There is udder chaos!

Where do you keep a pet vampire fish?

In your blood stream!

Doctor, doctor, I think I'm a cat!

How long have you felt like this?

Since I was a kitten!

What jobs are spiders good at?

Web designing!

What do you call a dog that thinks
it's a sheep?

Baa-king mad!

How do you help
Frankenstein's monster?

**Give him a hand
when he needs it!**

What sort of net
is useless for
catching fish?

A football net!

Why is it dangerous to tell jokes to Humpty Dumpty?

He might crack up!

What is the fairy tale about a girl who falls in love
with a really ugly loaf of bread?

Beauty and the yeast!

What is big and grey and has yellow feet?

An elephant standing in custard!

What is grey and highly dangerous?

An elephant with a hand grenade!

What do you call a dog that can operate
a farmer's four-wheel drive?

A Land Rover!

What do you call a rodent's favourite meal?

Ratatouille!

What do you call a rodent with a sword?

A mouseketeer!

What do you call a woman who has
lots of men at her feet?

A chiropodist!

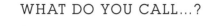

What do you call a woman with frog on her head?

Lily!

What do you call a sloth's favourite drink?

Ice-cream slowda!

What do you call a smelly giant gorilla?

King Pong!

What do you call a sweet-smelling
teddy bear?

Scented!

What do you call a posh car for butchers?

A sausage Rolls!

What do you call a pig with fangs?

A hampire!

What do you call
an embarrassed potato?

A beetroot!

What do you call a cross between a chicken and a dog?

Pooched eggs!

What do you call keep fit for ghosts?

Exorcise!

What do you call a woman who knows
where she lives?

Olivia!

What do you call a rabbit dressed up as a cake?

A cream bun!

What do you call a rock climbing teddy bear?

Mounted!

What do you call a happy teddy bear?

Contented!

What does a whale call the youngest member
of the family?

Her baby blubber!

What do you call two rows of cabbages?

A dual cabbageway!

What do you call an owl that robs the rich
and gives to the poor?

Robin Hoot!

What do you call a woman who fell off a cliff?

Eileen Dover!

What do you call a film about wildfowl?

A duck-umentary!

What do you call a place where cats and dogs
go to get new tails?

A retailer!

What do you call a flying skunk?

A smellicopter!

WHAT DO YOU CALL...?

What do you call the leader of a convent
who conquers the world?

Attila the Nun!

What do you call a burglar who fell into
a cement mixer?

A hardened criminal!

What do you call a baby crab?

A nipper!

What do you call something with 22 legs, eleven
heads and two wings?

A football team!

What do you call the ghost who's a member
of the Royal Family?

The Prince of Wails!

What do you call a TV programme
about a group of sheep?

A flock-umentary!

What do you call a bee who is always complaining?

A grumble bee!

What do you call a parrot when it has dried itself
after a bath?

Polly unsaturated!

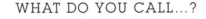

What do you call a dentist in the army?

A drill sergeant!

What do you call the illness that martial arts experts suffer from?

Kung Flu!

What do you call a girl who gets up very early in the morning?

Dawn!

What do you call someone who draws funny pictures of motor vehicles?

A car-toonist!

What do you call a fish on a motorcycle?

A motor pike!

What do you call a pen with no hair?

A bald point!

What do you call a magical secret agent?

James Wand!

What do you call a small parent?

A minimum!

What do you call the place where parrots
make films?

Pollywood!

What do you call a man with a plane parked
on his head?

Ron Way!